VITAL SIGNS

Deborah P Kolodji

Vital Signs

©2024 Deborah P Kolodji
All Rights Reserved

First Printing

ISBN 978-1-7350257-8-0

Cover photo by Tim Huntington, webnectar.com

CUTTLEFISH
BOOKS

ACKNOWLEDGEMENTS

Grateful appreciation is offered to the editors and publishers of *Acorn, Akitsu Quarterly, Blythe Spirit, bottle rockets, Chopin for Cherries Blog, California Quarterly, #FemkuMag, Frogpond, GEPPO, Haiku Canada Review, Haiku Dialogue, Haikuuniverse, Hedgerow, Heliosparrow, The Heron's Nest, Kingfisher, Kyoto Journal, Mariposa, Modern Haiku, Otata, Poetry Pea, Prune Juice, San Diego Poetry Annual 2019-2020, Stardust Haiku, tsuri-doro, Under the Basho,* as well as the anthologies *Against the Current* published by Moth Orchid Press and *A Moment's Longing* published by The Haiku Society of America, in which some of these poems have previously appeared or are forthcoming.

*for the wonderful women
of my cancer support group
and the doctors, nurses and staff
of USC Norris Cancer Hospital*

VITAL SIGNS

the blush of dawn
through a hospital window
vital signs

hospital bed
the blood pressure cuff
tightens

cold drizzle
windowless room
in the ER

December streets
the traffic flow
of rain

asterisks of steri-strips
a family's history
of breast cancer

dried prunes
I put on
my brave face

overripe loquats
the squished breasts
of a mammogram

sea star arms wide I sink into sand

the weight
of my indecision
standing water

hearing loss
my daughter's voice
turns into ocean

low tide
an ochre sea star clings
to the rock

hospital hair
the ghost
of who I am

dreams floating sea jellies

the parade
following my walker
hospital hall

unfilled prescription
for pain meds
winter desolation

hospital window
yesterday's flowers
on the window sill

hours swollen
with loneliness
colder days

alone
a nurse covers me
with a warmed blanket

if only my IV fluid
tasted like turkey
hospital Thanksgiving

ice chips
by my bedside
another thick book

as the shower drains
   I search for
     lumps

bamboo wind chimes
the hollow feeling
before prognosis

canopy of warblers our silence

sway
of hanging seed pods
autumn loneliness

fluid infusion
at the day hospital
the garden outside

gurgling fountain
in a rock cavity
cancer center

my day in slow motion koi

withered mums
never planted
breast cancer

CT scan journey to Mars

bear hibernation
the world inside
this hospital room

embarrassing moment
the nurse acts as if
he's seen it before

whistleblower PET scan

biopsy moon
the hoot owl haunts me
all night long

the traffic home
from the hospital
winter rainbow

extra weight
suddenly an advantage
chemotherapy

sturgeon moon
my pillowcase covered
with fallen hair

wheelchair those Martian rovers

away from all
I've ever known
fallen camellia

Ansel Adams photographs
in hospital halls
my life on hold

his old toolbox
no way to fix
all that's broken

Chopin étude
your fingers feel
my sadness

the cuff cold as I check
morning blood pressure
potted amaryllis

house finches
at the feeder
cancer support group

roof icicles
my fingers numb
from chemo

the nurse hums
taking my blood pressure
summertime

beige curtains
between infusion chairs
my shrinking world

the number of petals
on a daisy
another MRI

popcorn quilt
a doctor tries to outsmart
the cancer

rapid growth
of bougainvillea
thorns in my life

unresolved issues
the black hole in the center
of our galaxy

weeds after rain
a mailbox filled
with medical bills

Christmas catalogs
all the things
I will never order

bent lily stems
the wheelchair
in the corner

swallowtails
my own private
ghosts

white carpet
of plum blossoms
second chemo round

raccoon face
my teary eyes
after treatment

long wait
a stray pianist plays
the hospital piano

blue skipper
fluttering fluttering
shoulder pain

not yet extinct
the rainbow sheen
of another oil spill

leonid streaks across the sky promises

emerging
from tangled dreams
first blackberries

chair exercises
a squirrel
on a park bench

gray day
the cloudburst
on my pillow

a ship blocks
the Suez Canal
constipation

another week
of visiting the hospital
spring melancholy

wildflowers in bloom
when your children
take care of you

my cane-assisted gait
the awkward flight
of pelicans

long crooked road
a coyote's lament
at sunset

another pot
of geraniums
my doctor's bias

park bench
a skipper butterfly
sits awhile

ebb and flow
of my fear
dark ocean

mackerel sky
I catch a glimpse
of hope

hints of gray
in the sage leaves
my chemo hair

9-1-1 call
the side effects
of a rainy day

eucalyptus scent
another thousand
monarchs

murky water
a turtle scrambles over
the fallen palm

mallard ripples
my troubles fade
into the lake

forest stillness
condors return
to the Redwoods

AUTHOR'S NOTE

Being a cancer patient is like walking a tightrope, the journey is precarious and the slightest misstep, complication, side effect, or cancer mutation can cause you to lose your balance. Fortunately, I have had a safety net on this journey and I'm grateful for the family and friends who have been there for me, cooking dinners, taking me to appointments, and just generally being there. I am also thankful for the women of my cancer support group, who understand my journey because they are living similar journeys, listen, offer suggestions and have helped me keep a positive outlook. The members of the haiku community have also been supportive, nurturing my creativity, and I'm indebted to the wonderful doctors, nurses, and staff at USC Norris Cancer Hospital for their excellent care.

I chose a photo of a California Condor for the cover of this book because it embodies "Vital Signs" in a different way. In the early 1980's, right after I graduated from college, I became aware that the condor was teetering on the edge of extinction, with a living population of about two dozen birds. Those who were left were rounded up, removed from the wild, and taken to the Los Angeles Zoo and other zoo partners to be bred in captivity. As numbers grew in the captive breeding programs, birds began to be re-introduced into the wild in the early 1990's. As of December 2022, the population was at 561 birds, with 347 living in the wild.

I see the condor as a metaphor for cancer patients. Just as the condor came back from near extinction, cancer patients are also fighting for their own survival. Condors are tagged, which reminds me of hospital bracelets.

There are many types of struggles we all face, so I'm hoping these poems will resonate with you on your own life journey.

Finally, thanks to Cuttlefish Books for publishing this book.

Deborah P Kolodji

www.ingramcontent.com/pod-product-compliance
Lightning Source LLC
Chambersburg PA
CBHW061739070526
44585CB00024B/2744

ABOUT THE AUTHOR

Deborah P Kolodji is the moderator of the Southern California Haiku Study Group, the California Regional Coordinator for the Haiku Society of America, a member of the board of directors for Haiku North America, and the former president of the Science Fiction and Fantasy Poetry Association. A native Californian, she has a degree in mathematics from the University of Southern California. With over 1000 published haiku to her name, her first full-length book of haiku and senryu, *highway of sleeping towns*, from Shabda Press, was awarded a Touchstone Distinguished Book Award from The Haiku Foundation. Her e-chapbook, *tug of a black hole* from Title IX Press, won 2nd Place in the Elgin Awards from the Science Fiction and Fantasy Poetry Association. Her latest book, a collection of Tan-ku written with Tokyo tanka poet Mariko Kitakubo was published by Shabda Press. She finds inspiration in the beaches, mountains, deserts, gardens, and urban life of Los Angeles County.